Amazing God Stories

Inspirational Christian Stories of
Miracles from God

Jordy Christo

Copyright

Jordy Christo
Copyright, Legal Notice and Disclaimer:

Copyright Notices:

NIV

Table of Contents

Introduction

These short stories will fill you with faith and renew your hope in knowing that God is near.

A quote from a Newsboys song: "God's not dead, he's surely alive".

As you read, it's the author's desire that you will see with clarity how supernatural things can occur in an instant to set the course of God's will for your life.

These real life stories testify that Jesus Christ is alive and the Holy Spirit is working mightily in the earth.

The Lord loves you and desires to demonstrate His miracle working power in your life.

The Night I Was Saved for Real

During my teenage years, I'd been heading in the wrong direction for a couple of years, drinking, smoking pot and doing the idiotic things that 15 and 16 year olds do. I didn't grow up in a Christian family and had no interest in attending church. At age 16, I found myself very attracted to a young lady in my neighborhood. One Sunday afternoon, I got up the nerve to ask her if she would like to go to the movies. In turn, she invited me to attend her youth group instead because they were having a special guest that night. My heart was elated as I agreed to go with her, not because it was church, but because she was very beautiful.

God had lured me in for the catch and I'd taken the bait.

The special guest was a guy in his early thirties. He was playing an acoustic guitar and singing to the group of us teens at a Vamo United Methodist Church in Sarasota, Fl. Long story short, that night I met God for real when the singer gave an altar call. The Holy Spirit was so heavy on me that I literally crawled from the second pew in front of the church all the way to the altar, located at the base of the stage. That was 35 years ago and I'm still in the palm of the Lord's hand.

For weeks, the Holy Spirit was very tangible throughout every minute of the day. I started reading the Bible and would spend every night before I went to bed conversing with the Lord. I was falling deeply in love with Christ at a very fast pace.

I stopped drinking and quit smoking both cigarettes and pot. My foul mouth disappeared and the old me was swiftly fading away.

2 Corinthians 5:17 (NIV) Therefore, if anyone is in Christ, the new creation has come: The old has gone, the new is here!

It was about two months after being saved that I took an interest in learning how to play the acoustic guitar.

When God Calls You

A kid in my neighborhood had started taking guitar lessons and I took an interest in it. He told me that the studio where he was taking lessons rented guitars to students. The whole idea sounded affordable to me. So, I decided to give guitar lessons a try.

After about two months of taking guitar lessons, I had learned the basic open chords and had begun learning bar chords. At this point, I was getting a little discouraged because my fingers were just not cooperating with the positioning of the bar chords. If you've ever reached this point in guitar lessons, you know exactly what I am talking about.

I was also very discouraged as to how my guitar playing was going in comparison to that of my friend. In my eyes, his guitar playing appeared to be incredible whereas mine was mediocre.

It was during the first couple of months of learning to play that I discovered a very intimate connection with God through worshipping with an original song. It was my first song ever and the only lyrics were, "I know you're here Lord, I know you are here..." That's it; there were no more words, but I sang them along with a three chord progression with all of my heart. I really knew God was near.

James 4:8 Come near to God and he will come near to you. Wash your hands, you sinners, and purify your hearts, you double-minded.

Prior to a guitar lesson, I sat outside the studio, under some tall pine trees, in my little green Datsun 1200. The bar chords had really taken a toll on my inspiration to continue playing the guitar and my insecurities were really working me over. I was very seriously considering quitting guitar lessons. For a brief moment I prayed: "Lord, if you want me to continue taking guitar lessons, please give me a sign."

I went into the studio and had my lesson. When we finished, I was so excited about the song I'd written, I asked my guitar teacher if I could play and sing it for him. He agreed. I'm sure I sang those five words with all of the passion I had inside of me because every time I would sing "I know you're here Lord, I know you are here," I felt as if God were right there with me, hugging and holding me close. There was a thick and tangible presence of the Lord every time I would sing the song.

When I went to pay the teacher for the guitar lesson, it was time to pay the monthly fee for the guitar rental. I handed him the money for both and he handed me back the money for the guitar rental and told me that he wanted me to have the guitar.

WOW, WOW, WOW! Talk about God answering your prayers. That was when I knew that my special calling in life was to do something with music.

1 Corinthians 2:9 (KJV) But as it is written, Eye hath not seen, nor ear heard, neither have entered into the heart of man, the things which God hath prepared for them that love him.

That occurred in 1979; I'm writing this book in 2014. Since then, I've had the opportunity to bless so many people through the music that the Lord has entrusted me with. I've written a pile of songs, recorded a couple of CDs, worked as a youth worship leader and led worship services for thousands of people.

To date, I know of two people who have personally told me that during a time when I was leading worship, God healed them of being deaf in one ear. I've observed hundreds of people through the years with tears streaming down their faces while I've been singing. Countless lives have been touched by the Holy Spirit, through the gift of music that God has entrusted me with. God is truly amazing.

An Amazing Fulfillment of Prophecy in My Life

As a new Christian, I started attending church on a regular basis. Of course I stayed for a while at the Methodist Church in which I'd been saved, but then I followed the Lord's lead into a non-denominational church that was a bit more charismatic.

One Sunday evening, pastor Sherman Owens, our assistant pastor, was preaching. I was sitting in the second row back from the front of the church. Right in the middle of Pastor Sherman's message, he pointed right at me and said, "Jordy, come here."

As I made my way to the front of the church, I felt the presence of the Lord getting stronger, or maybe it was stage fright kicking in. He told me to stand in front of him. Pastor Sherman then proceeded to look right at me, started speaking in a heavenly language and then gave an interpretation.

What the Lord did through what he prophesied is more than incredible. When you finish reading this chapter, you will be as amazed as I was then and still am now, 35 years later.

The paraphrased version of what the pastor prophesied for my life goes something like this: "Jordy, the Lord is going to give you a youth ministry and it's going to be on a very large scale." He said a lot of things that night, but in my heart, I came away with exactly what the previous sentence says. This happened in 1979 when I was about 17 years old. At time of writing I am now 52 years old.

After that night and for the next 30 years, I periodically wondered if Pastor Sherman had missed the mark or if the choices I'd made in life were not in line with the will of God. There was actually a time when I strayed away from the Lord, but He never let me go. Anyway, over the years, there was no youth ministry on a large scale. In fact, I was not involved in any kind of youth ministry over the years.

Then something started to happen and I never even saw it coming. I was in my mid 40s and participating in a street ministry through my church. Every other Friday evening, a small group of us would go downtown where teens gathered near the movie theater. Our purpose was to be witnesses for Christ and to talk to people about their spiritual lives.

One night as I was talking to two teenagers, I had a thought that came from out of nowhere: to start a website where teens can send in prayer requests. I knew that God had spoken to me, but I didn't know the first thing about building websites. Actually,

I didn't know diddley about computer stuff. Regardless, in response to the strong thought I heard, I instantly said to myself, "God, if that was you, You'll have to make this happen because I don't have a clue as to how to build a website." I didn't have the money to pursue the idea either.

About one year later, I hired a friend to build a music website for me so I could share my original music with the world. This was right about the time when Google was becoming the king of the Internet, YouTube was newly established and people everywhere were starting to move toward the world of the Internet. Cell phones were beginning to transform into mini computers and the digital world was exploding with new ideas.

The website building program package which my friend used to build my music website allowed unlimited sites to be built. It was my account, so I could have as many sites on it as I desired. All I had to do was purchase a domain name to connect to the site.

One night, I asked my friend if I could try to build a website. He said sure and gave me full access to the site builder and some instructions on how to get started. There were tutorial videos that I watched and it wasn't long, only a couple of hours, before I actually had a horrid web page built. The creative side of my personality was hooked on a desire to build websites.

A few days later, as I was practicing building random web pages in order to get familiar with the program, the Holy Spirit reminded me of the words He had planted in my heart a couple of years earlier: "start a website where teens can send in prayer requests."

Right now as I am writing, tears have just filled my eyes with deep-felt appreciation and gratitude for what the Lord has done.

Keep reading and you will be amazed, I promise!

I called my friend and asked him how to get a domain name. He explained things to me and within a day, I had purchased "PrayerForYouth.com."

Within a couple of weeks, I had the website up on the Internet and to my amazement, the traffic statistics were showing that I was getting a couple of visitors per day. Without boring you with drawn out details, let's just say God made the right connections over the next few months and the traffic to the site increased steadily.

I asked a female friend, Lucy Ann, if she would handle all the prayer requests for the girls and she said yes. I took all the requests for the boys. As the months passed and I learned more about Internet promotions, the prayer requests steadily increased.

Within six months, the Lord led me to write daily devotions and put them on the site. I would write them five at a time, Lucy Ann would edit them and I'd post them on the site. I created an email subscription for youth to receive FREE daily devotions.

The response was good. Before long, I had an average of 10 people signing up for the free email devotions per day. The number of subscribers steadily increased as time went on.

Then the testimonials started coming in. I started getting emails from youth leaders telling me how much the devotions were helping them and their youth. Leaders would subscribe, receive the daily devotion and then send it out to their youth group teens. There was a dramatic multiplication taking place, with the devotions being distributed and shared beyond what I could see in my online statistics.

An amazing thing was happening with the daily devotions. I was getting testimonials from Christian school teachers and Sunday school teachers telling me how they were using the daily devotions in their classes as topics for discussion.

As this rapid growing process continued over the next year, I never even thought about the prophecy that the Lord had pastor

Sherman Owens speak regarding my life 23 years earlier. One day it hit me: this is what the pastor prophesied. "Jordy, the Lord is going to give you a youth ministry and it's going to be on a very large scale."

To date, that's to say, January 2014, Prayer For Youth sends out over 2 million emails every year with a daily devotion inside. The devotions go all over the world. Now if that's not a youth ministry on a large scale, I don't know what is. God is amazing!

2 Peter 1:21 (NIV) For prophecy never had its origin in the human will, but prophets, though human, spoke from God as they were carried along by the Holy Spirit.

The Box of Tide: An Amazing Miracle

I t was during a very dark time in my life when the Lord shined His love and light in amazing ways. I've always said that when the disciples were going through the most intense difficulties, that's when the Lord showed up in the most incredible ways.

Acts 12:7 (NIV) Suddenly an angel of the Lord appeared and a light shone in the cell. He struck Peter on the side and woke him up. "Quick, get up!" he said, and the chains fell off Peter's wrists.

I don't fully understand the way things were going in my life at the time this story was created. The one thing I do know is that God touched me in an amazing way in the midst of a very dark and confusing time. Actually, God touched me in so many ways in the midst of the darkness that words can hardly express how wonderful He is.

I'm going to make this short without a lot of details. Nonetheless, I am sure you will be dazzled by the amazing miracle that happened to me. This miracle of God will amaze you as much as it did me.

I was in a relationship that was going very sour. It was a marriage headed toward divorce. I'd been enduring my wife's unacceptable behavior for a very long time while hoping, praying and standing in faith that things would change.

At one time when the tension in the home had been escalating for about a week, my wife ended up in jail on domestic violence charges. The following morning I was filled with every conceivable emotion you can imagine. My marriage was falling apart and my wife was in jail. I had full responsibility for a 2800 sq. ft. home, children, pets and a business. I was sad, angry, depressed, hopeless, hopeful, confused and desperate to hear from God.

For several days leading up to this, we had been out of laundry detergent and there was a gigantic pile of clothes in the laundry room.

I started my day frantically and desperately praying, asking God what He wanted me to do. I was literally an emotional wreck. As I was pacing back and forth in my bedroom, alone, praying fervently, I felt so strongly in my spirit that I was supposed to do the laundry.

My kids had gone to school, my wife was in jail, my marriage was falling apart and God directed me to do the laundry. Now that may sound very strange, but inside my spirit, I knew what God was telling me to do.

I was self-employed at the time and was operating a cabinet manufacturing business from my home. There were many things to do that morning concerning the business along with other things including filing a restraining order, etc.

Long story short, every time I would leave the house to run an errand, I would think, "I'll get laundry detergent while I'm out, so I can do the laundry." As you can imagine, I was having a horrible time concentrating on anything that day.

I would go out to run an errand and forget to get laundry detergent. I'd get back to the house and sigh as I said to myself, "When I go out next time, I'll get the laundry detergent."

Stay with me on this story because God did the most amazing thing.

Finally, after going out to run errands and coming home without laundry detergent for about the fifth or sixth time, I got really irritated. On the last trip, when I returned without remembering to get the soap, I walked in the front door of my house, realized I'd forgotten to get the detergent, SLAMMED DOWN my briefcase on the floor and turned completely around and flung open the front door!

I WAS NOW ON A MISSION! I was going straight to the store for one purpose and one purpose only: to get laundry detergent. I was frustrated with myself and aggressively heading out the door.

As I walked down the front porch steps, I looked down toward the long sidewalk leading to the driveway.

What did I see? Coming toward me was a man, a total stranger, holding something in his left hand. His arm was bent and the box was at shoulder height. We walked toward each other. As I got closer, I could clearly see what the box was.

WOW, WOW, WOW! He was holding a small box of Tide laundry detergent. My eyes must have been as big as tennis balls. I asked the stranger, "Is that laundry detergent for me?"

The stranger replied, "Yes, if you will allow me to do a demonstration of my product, you can have the detergent. Actually, I have several different kinds in my car you can choose from if you don't like this brand."

I didn't realize at the time everything that the Lord was telling me. All I knew is that God was letting me know that he knew my every thought and he knew my every need. I realized that God could deliver exactly what I needed when I needed it.

So, for the next two years of going through a separation and divorce, I was provided for in miraculous ways. Just as the box of Tide was delivered to my door, I experienced God's supernatural support within my life.

I had an attorney who didn't require a retainer fee (I was able to remodel her kitchen and bathroom cabinets along with the restrooms in the law firm as payment for her services). God had provided exactly the right attorney and a means for paying my bills.

When the time came for me to move out of the house, I was provided a place where I could have lived rent free, but chose to pay a small amount in rent on the advice of my attorney. The house the Lord provided was a beautiful four bedroom home, on a lake with a pool. The house was the second home of a friend of mine who I hadn't known for very long.

When I moved in, I stayed in a spare bedroom. Once I had earned Bob and Ruth's trust, they actually let me take care of the house for about sixteen months while they were at their other home in Louisville, Kentucky. They paid for everything while I stayed at their home: the water bill, the cable bill, the Internet service, the lawn service, the pool service and all of the maintenance on the home. During this time, I was able to finish the divorce proceedings without a tremendous amount of financial pressure and save some money. God is amazing!

When it came time for me to move out, I sensed strongly in my spirit that I'd saved enough money for the first, last and security payment needed to get a new apartment. Once I'd secured my new place, I would have no money left for the required furniture. For some reason, I wasn't worried about not having furniture. There was a God given faith inside of me that everything would work out fine.

The same weekend I planned on moving into my apartment, a new friend of mine was moving out of his house and into a smaller place, and needed some place to store his furniture.

The short version of the story is that I furnished my whole apartment with a living room set, dining room set and master bedroom set and it didn't cost me a thing. This was very nice furniture too, not junk, but practically new. The day that my friend had to move the furniture out of his house was the exact same day I had planned to move into my apartment.

Now, my friend was actually just letting me use the furnishings until he got a place large enough to move into. As things in his life went differently than he planned, he eventually ended up giving me all of the furniture. God is amazing!

Not long after I moved into the apartment, my Ford Bronco was running horribly and soon on its way to the junkyard. One night when it was really cold, a friend of mine was visiting me at my apartment and upon leaving, I walked him out to the parking lot. We walked by the Bronco and I told him that my kids would be cold in the morning on the way to school because the heater in the Bronco wasn't working (plus, the rear window was busted out).

My friend looked at me and said, "Jordy, I wasn't sure when I was going to tell you this, but I think now is the time. I know the Lord wants me to give you my Jeep."

"WHAT!!!!" I exclaimed. Over the next couple of days we took care of the formalities and then I was driving a really nice white Jeep Grand Cherokee. The funny thing is that about two years prior to this happening, I had been looking specifically for a white Jeep. My friend didn't know about my heart's desire; only God knew about that one. God is amazing!

Matthew 7:11 (NIV) If you, then, though you are evil, know how to give good gifts to your children, how much more will your Father in heaven give good gifts to those who ask him!

As you can see, the box of Tide was a prophetic promise from the Lord. I feel that because the Lord delivered laundry detergent to my door, He was telling me that there were some things that we're going to be cleaned up in my life. The Lord also communicated with the delivery of the detergent that He would provide what I needed, exactly when I needed it. He did provide for me in miraculous ways as my life was dramatically changed because of my (or the) divorce.

Without saying a lot about how bad things had gotten in the marriage, let me just say that I had relied on God's promises, believing in change for a long time. I held firmly to the scripture that states God hates divorce.

I don't understand why things turned out the way they did. Perhaps God knew that things were not going to change in the relationship. I do know this: God delivered me from a very abusive situation and he did it in miraculous ways, in ways that only God could have done.

I still hold firm to the scripture that states God hates divorce. Nonetheless, I can say that God loves me more than he hates divorce.

The Parachute Dream

After reading the previous story, you now know that I went through a divorce. Not long after things were finalized, I started attending a divorce recovery group at my church.

One night, while I was sleeping, I had a dream. In the dream there was a man from my divorce recovery group named John. John's face was as clear and real looking as if I had been face to face with him in real life.

The Dream:

I was standing in a very large empty warehouse, when suddenly, John was face to face with me, telling me that I had to fix the parachute that was behind me on the floor and put it on so that I could get to the second floor. I sensed that there was a party on the second floor. It was a joyous celebration of single people having an exuberant time. In the next part of the dream, I was kneeling, trying to fix the parachute, got frustrated because I couldn't, stood up and turned around to see a fireman's pole. I grabbed the pole and was instantly whisked up to the second floor. That was the end of the dream.

I have a very close friend who does dream interpretations based on biblical truths. He has had a lot of training in this area, but more importantly, he has a relationship with God that is closer than that of anyone I know. He loves the Lord greatly and I have faith in his abilities to hear what the Holy Spirit is saying.

My friend interpreted the dream with the statement, "the way up is down." Then he explained that the Lord was telling me that in order to reach higher levels of joy, I should be spending time on my knees in prayer.

The two things in the dream that were there to bring me upward to the second floor, the parachute and fireman's pole, are actually things which are used to help people go down. In the dream, I was kneeling in order to repair the parachute.

There were other meanings of the dream, but I want you to connect with the phrase "the way up is down."

A couple of nights after my friend did the interpretation, I attended my divorce recovery class. When the class was over, we were all socializing in the room. I had my back turned on John (the man in the dream who told me to fix the parachute). He was talking to someone behind me. All of the sudden, I heard John say to the person he was talking to, "the way up is down."

Wow! I took that as a confirmation that the dream had been interpreted correctly. I spent a lot of time on my knees in prayer after having that dream. God is amazing.

Wait, there's more to this story.

Fast forward to about seven years later: Here I am leading worship for a conference in my home town. There are about 100 to 200 people attending. When the church service ended, a total stranger walked up to me and introduced himself.

"Hi, my name is Garth. You don't know me, but sometimes I have visions. Your pastor knows me and can vouch that what I am saying is true, that the Lord allows me to see things others can't. I'm not sure what this means, but I feel strongly that the Lord wants me to share this with you. While you were leading worship, the Lord gave me a clear vision of you. All I saw was you kneeling in a large warehouse repairing a parachute.

Wow, wow, wow! Can you believe that? God loves me so much to remind me that he knows exactly where I am and exactly where I have been. The Lord was bringing comfort to me by saying through Garth, "I was with you then and I'm with you now."

Jeremiah 29:11 (NIV) "For I know the plans I have for you," declares the Lord, "plans to prosper you and not to harm you, plans to give you hope and a future."

The Nurse from 500 Miles Away

This is going to be a really short story. I'm not sure why things happened this way. I honestly have no explanation or even deep spiritual insight. One thing I do know is that God did what I am about to share with you; there's no doubt in my mind that He arranged things to happen the way they did.

When my first daughter was born, it was a long process of induced labor. My wife had been in labor for a while when a new nurse entered the small room. She picked up the chart and said, "Your last name is Christo. Are you related to George Christo who lives in Panama City, Fl.?" (which was almost 500 miles away from where we were at the moment of her asking).

I said, "Yes, he's my uncle." She told me that she was friends with George. Then the most amazing thing happened. She shared with us that she met George because she was the private nurse that came into my grandmother's home and cared for her when she was dying. You see, my grandparents were very wealthy and could afford to have this type of home care.

The nurse's name was Judy. Since Judy felt such an amazing connection with us as we did with her, she decided to stay overtime and extend her shift until the baby was born.

I honestly don't know why God arranged for the same nurse that cared for my grandmother, who lived 500 miles away, to be sent to help deliver my baby. It's a mystery to me. One thing I do know is that as I am writing this, the tears are streaming down my face as I am reminded of how utterly amazing God is.

A Stranger Tells Me What's Going to Happen

When the papers had been filed and we were headed toward divorce, we couldn't live in the house together anymore. The tension was just too immense. As you recall from my Tide story, I had a cabinet manufacturing business that I was operating from the house. It was actually in the two car garage where I was manufacturing kitchens, vanities and furniture.

It was on a Sunday when I met a man at a barbecue named Rick. I was scheduled to go to court on Monday and the judge was going to decide who would get to live in the house while the divorce was being finalized.

The barbecue party was happening just down the street from my house. The host of the party asked if I could go to my house and get some ice because they were running out. I said sure. At the time of her asking, I was having a really good conversation with my new found friend of about three hours, Rick. I asked Rick if he would like to go with me. We went together to get the ice and quickly returned to the BBQ.

About three hours later, after Rick and I had been conversing most of the afternoon, we were sitting around the pool with a friend named Ron. We started talking about Godly things and radical God stories. I guess the more radical Ron and I got with our God stories, the more comfortable Rick became to share what follows.

Suddenly, Rick looks at me and says, "Jordy, there's something I need to tell you. I have been hesitant to share this with you ever since we went to your house to get ice because I didn't want you to think I was crazy. As soon as we pulled up to your house, I recognized it as the house that was in a dream that I had when I was about 10 years old (the dream had occurred 35 years prior in New Hampshire. The house wasn't even built then and is located in Florida). All I remember about the dream is that there was a man who was a cabinet maker and who was allowed to work at the house, but couldn't live there."

My instant response was "THAT'S NOT ME, MAN." I said that because I believed God would make a way for me to live in my house and eventually own it through the divorce proceedings. I believed the judge would order my wife to leave our house.

The following day came and here's what the judge said:

"Mr. Christo, you can come to work every day at the house at 7AM and must leave by 5PM. You will be allowed to work there

Monday through Friday, but you will not be able to live there. You will have full reign and access to the entire house while you are there. You may come and go as you please during your designated time. However, you will not live there. Please collect your things and be out of the house by 5:00 this afternoon."

John 16:13 But when he, the Spirit of truth, comes, he will guide you into all the truth. He will not speak on his own; he will speak only what he hears, and he will tell you what is yet to come.

That was difficult news to swallow, as I had believed that God would make a way for me to continue living there. The judge placed an order on my wife at the same time. He told her that she had to be away from the house during the times that I was granted to be there. This was due to the restraining order I had filed.

Nonetheless, God is truly amazing. In the middle of the largest storm I'd ever been in in life, God whispers through a stranger's dream that he knew many years before the house was built that I would be working there and not living there. God is amazing.

In the previous story about the box of Tide being delivered to my door, you read about the house that I lived in where the couple basically paid for my living expenses for a year and a half. That's the house I moved into when the judge ordered me to move out of my house. God took care of me in the middle of one of the most difficult times I've ever gone through in my life.

Psalms 23

1 The Lord is my shepherd; I shall not want.

2 He maketh me to lie down in green pastures: he leadeth me beside the still waters.

3 He restoreth my soul: he leadeth me in the paths of righteousness for his name's sake.

4 Yea, though I walk through the valley of the shadow of death, I will fear no evil: for thou art with me; thy rod and thy staff they comfort me.

5 Thou preparest a table before me in the presence of mine enemies: thou anointest my head with oil; my cup runneth over.

6 Surely goodness and mercy shall follow me all the days of my life: and I will dwell in the house of the Lord forever.

From The Author

Thank you for downloading and reading this book. You can help spread the good news of God's amazing love by leaving a positive review on the product page.

This book is the first of a series. Keep an eye out on Amazon for the next book scheduled to be released in November, 2016.

Blessings,
Jordy Christo

Made in the USA
Monee, IL
11 December 2022

20853361R00024